A LITTLE BIT OF TEXAS

Norma J Graves

ISBN-10: 1534735917
ISBN-13: 978-1533510372

DEDICATION

This coloring book is dedicated to my children and grandchildren.

Artist's Note

A ***Little Bit of Texas*** is hand-drawn representations of the beautiful flowers and atmosphere of the Texan culture presented for your relaxation and stress relief. We hope you take a little bit of time each day to enjoy yourself and relax.

This book has a sample of many of the plants and animals you will find growing wild along the roads, woodlands, and lakes of Texas.

Fill Your Boots With The Yellow Roses Of Texas And Your Heart With Love All The Days Of Your Life.

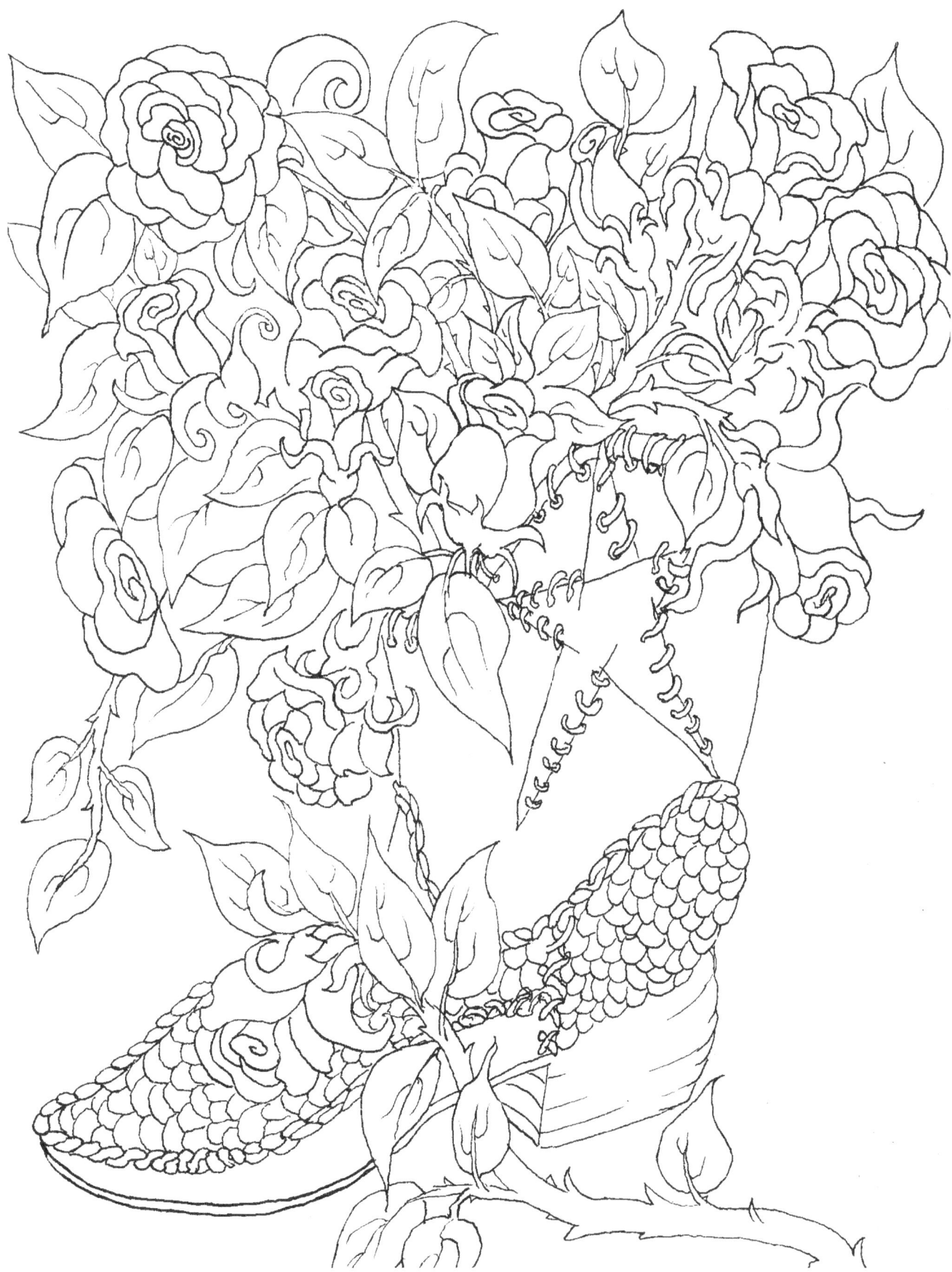

Find the diamond shapes. The more diamonds you find, the more people you love. Find the heart shapes. The more hearts you find, the more people that love you.

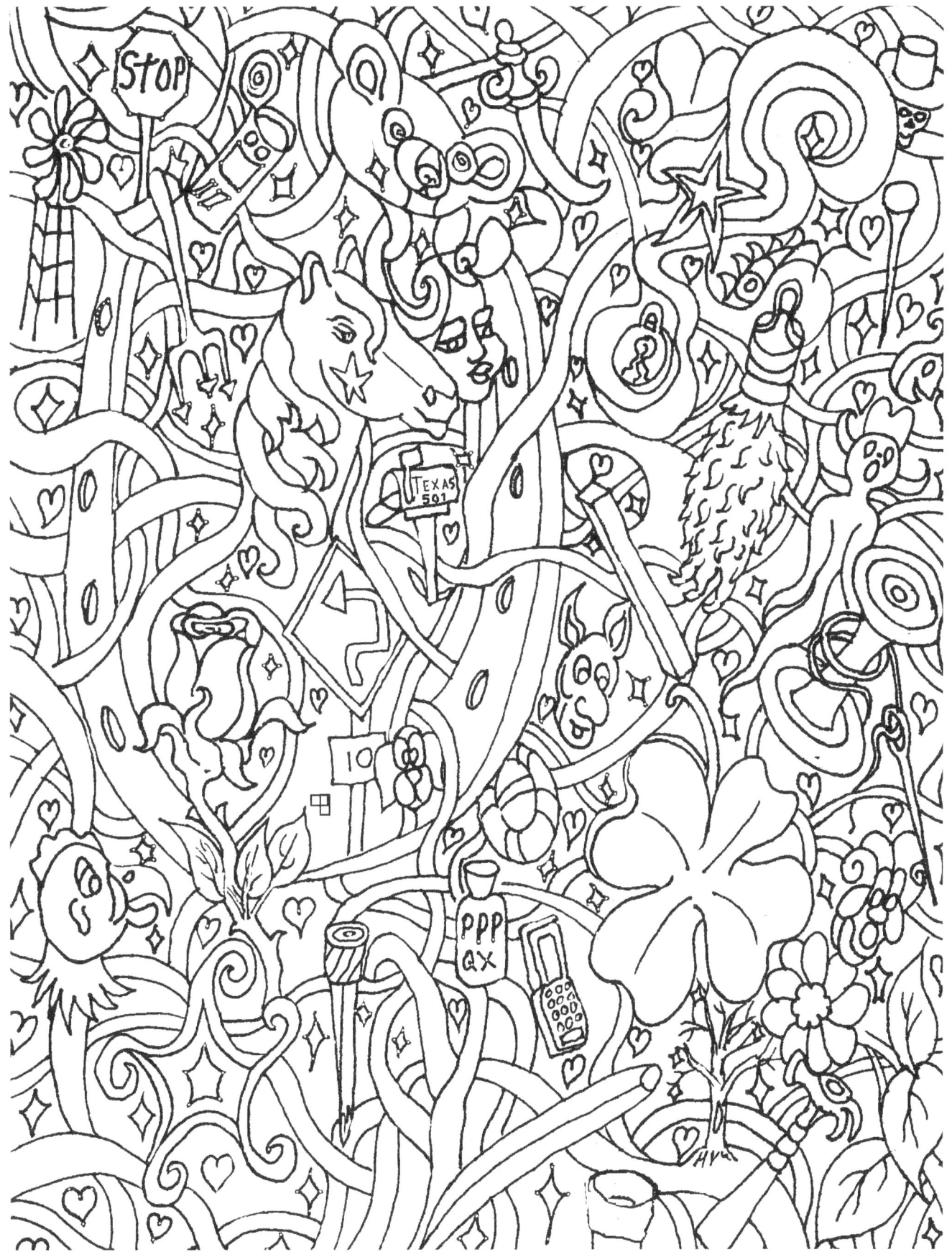

Everybody needs to howl at the moon sometimes!

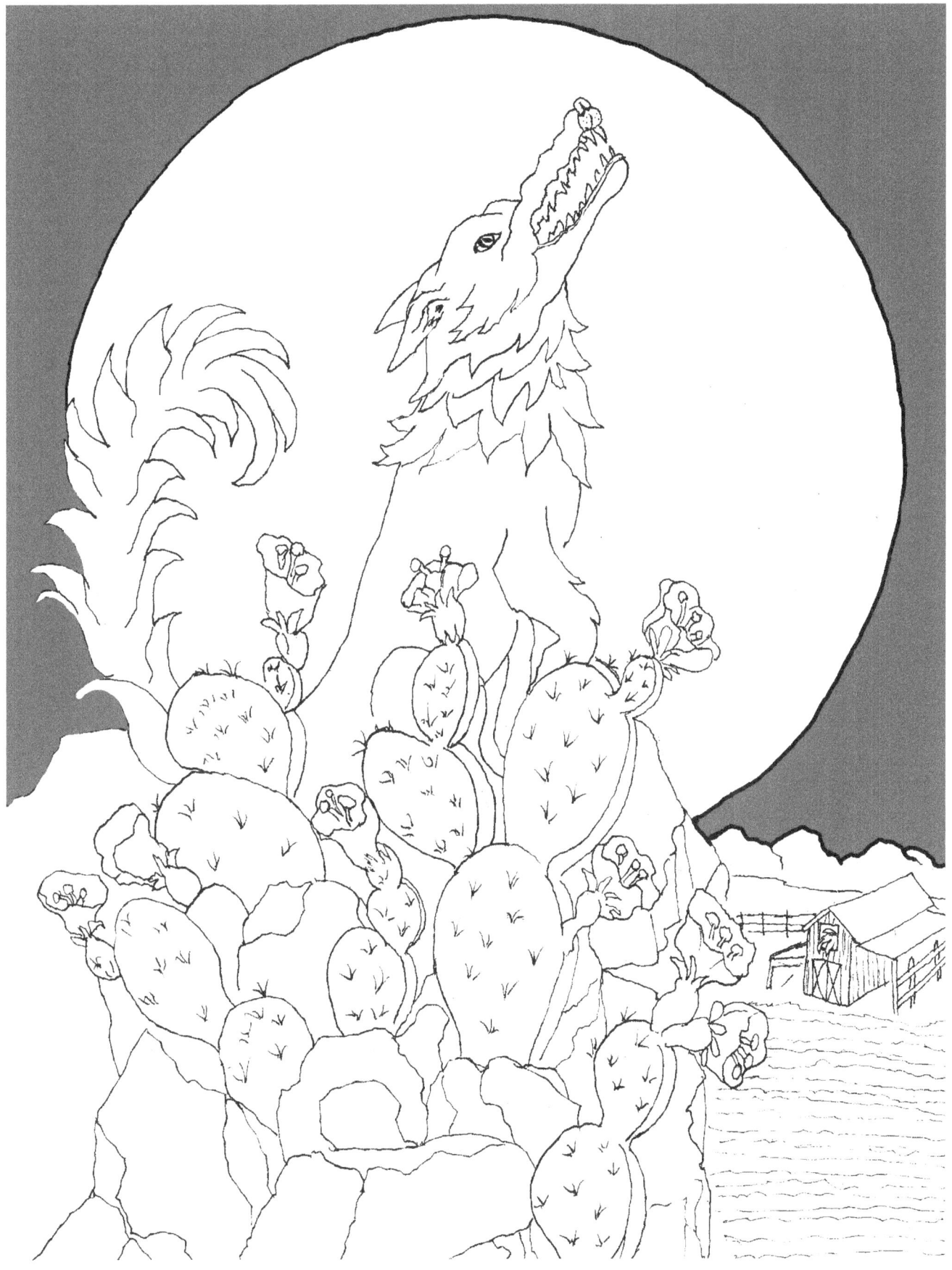

Who knows what the wise old owl knows?
I know!

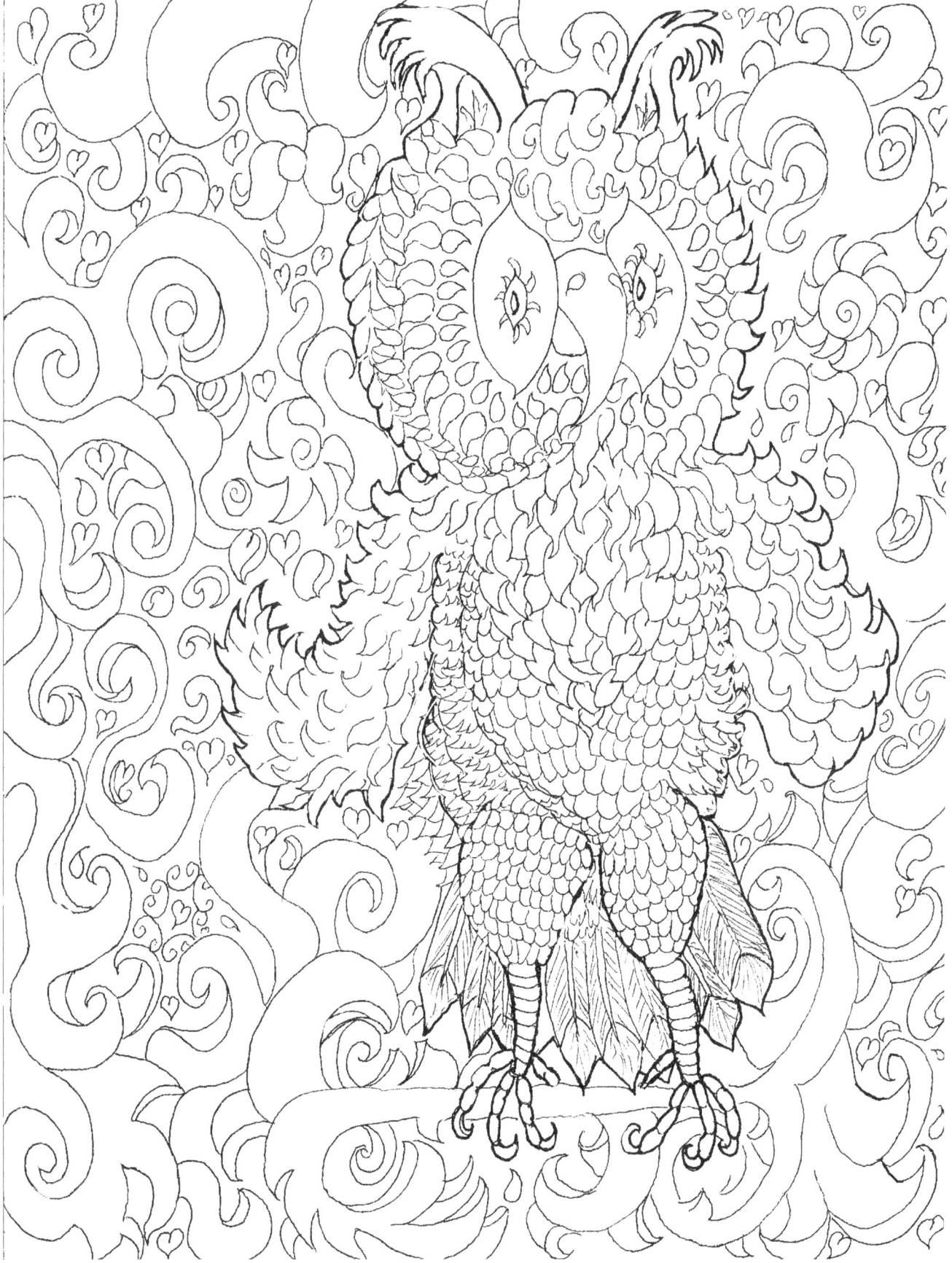

One of my grandbabies is all grown up. Isn't she beautiful?

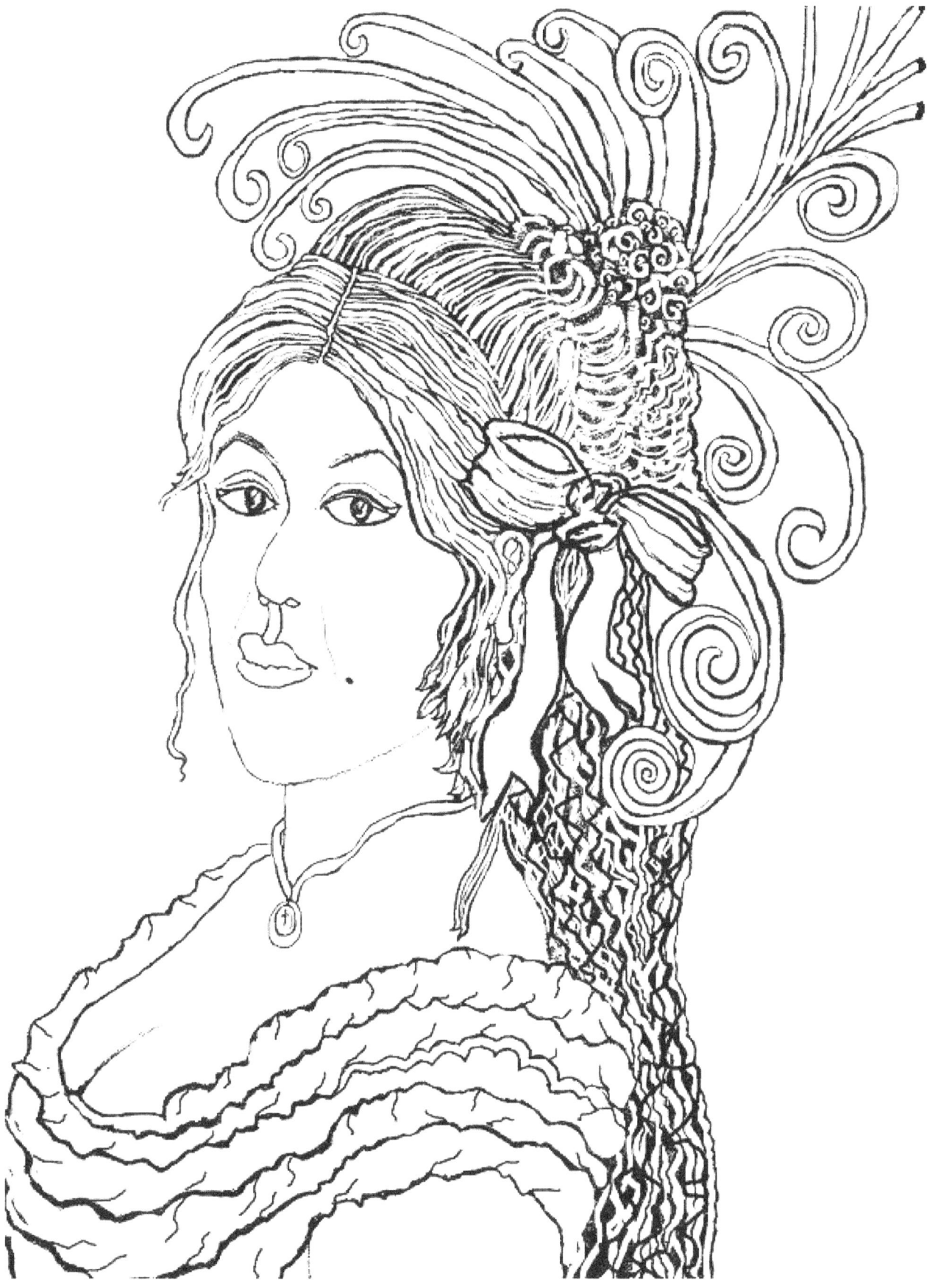

Deep in the woods near the morning glories, if you are lucky you might see an elusive lynx. If you are super lucky, you might see his friend the fairy.

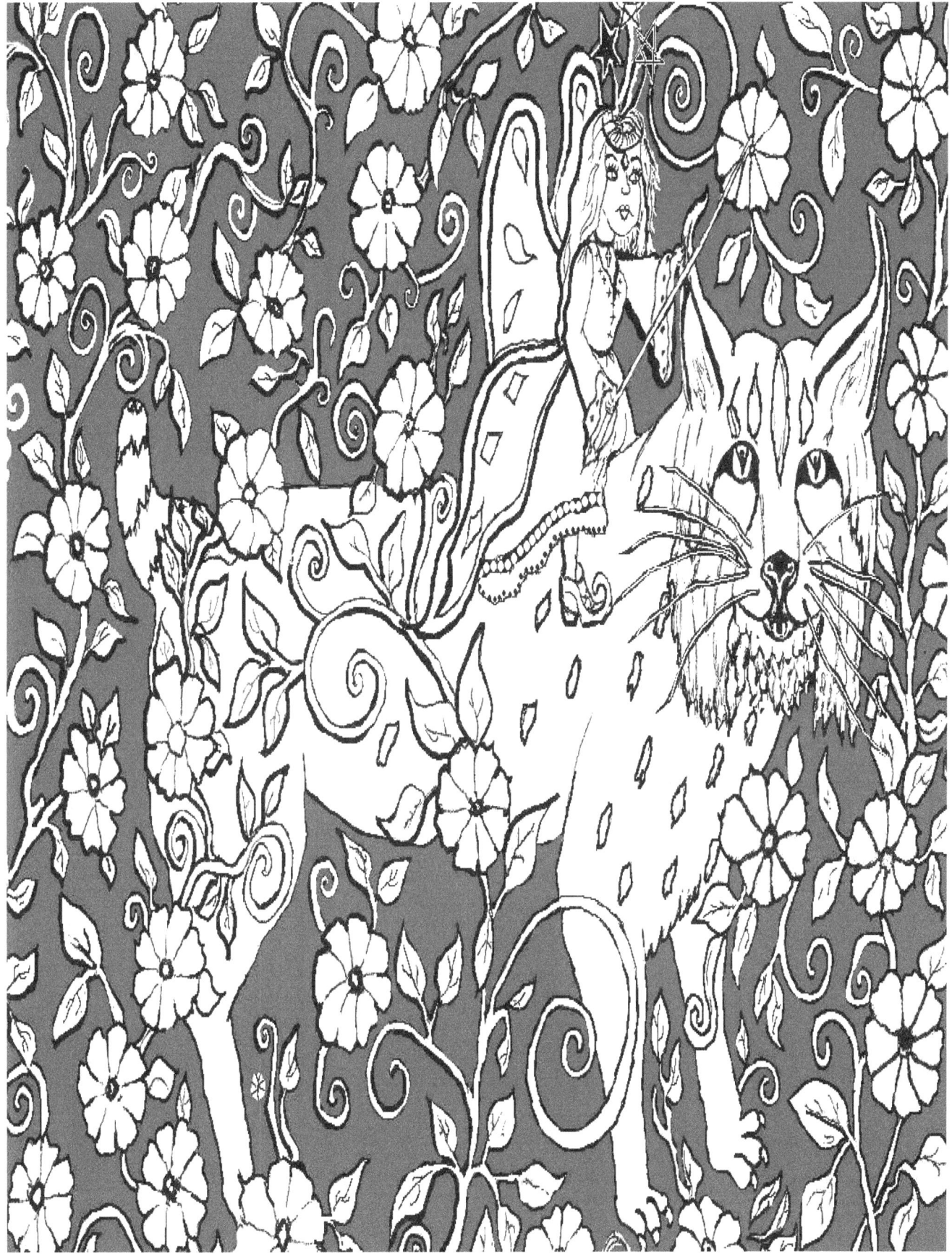

As you drive down the roads of Texas in the Springtime, the wildflowers planted by Ladybird Johnson will amaze you. Thank you, my Lady.

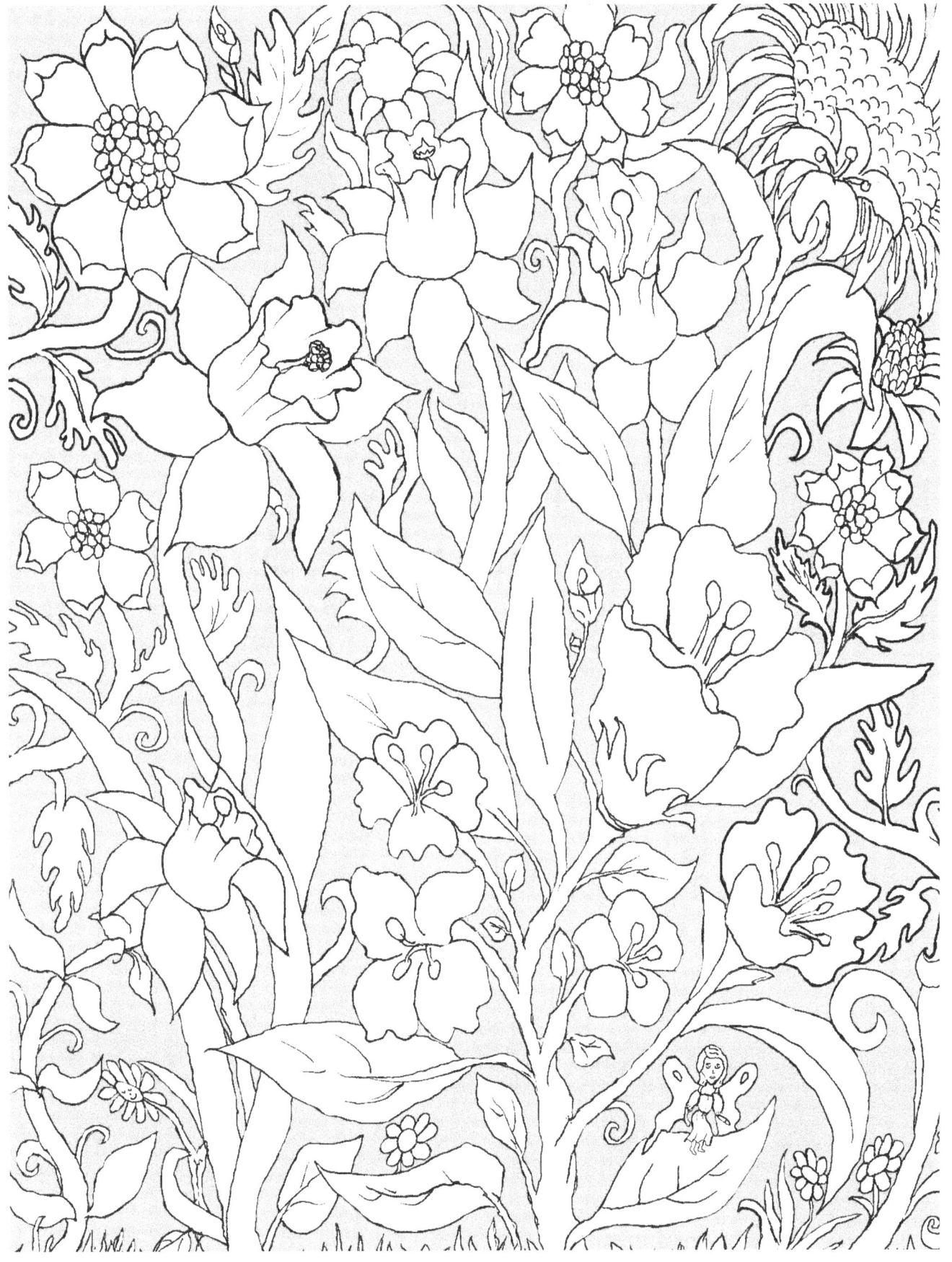

The happy sunflowers wake up to the morning sun and follows the sun from the East to the West.

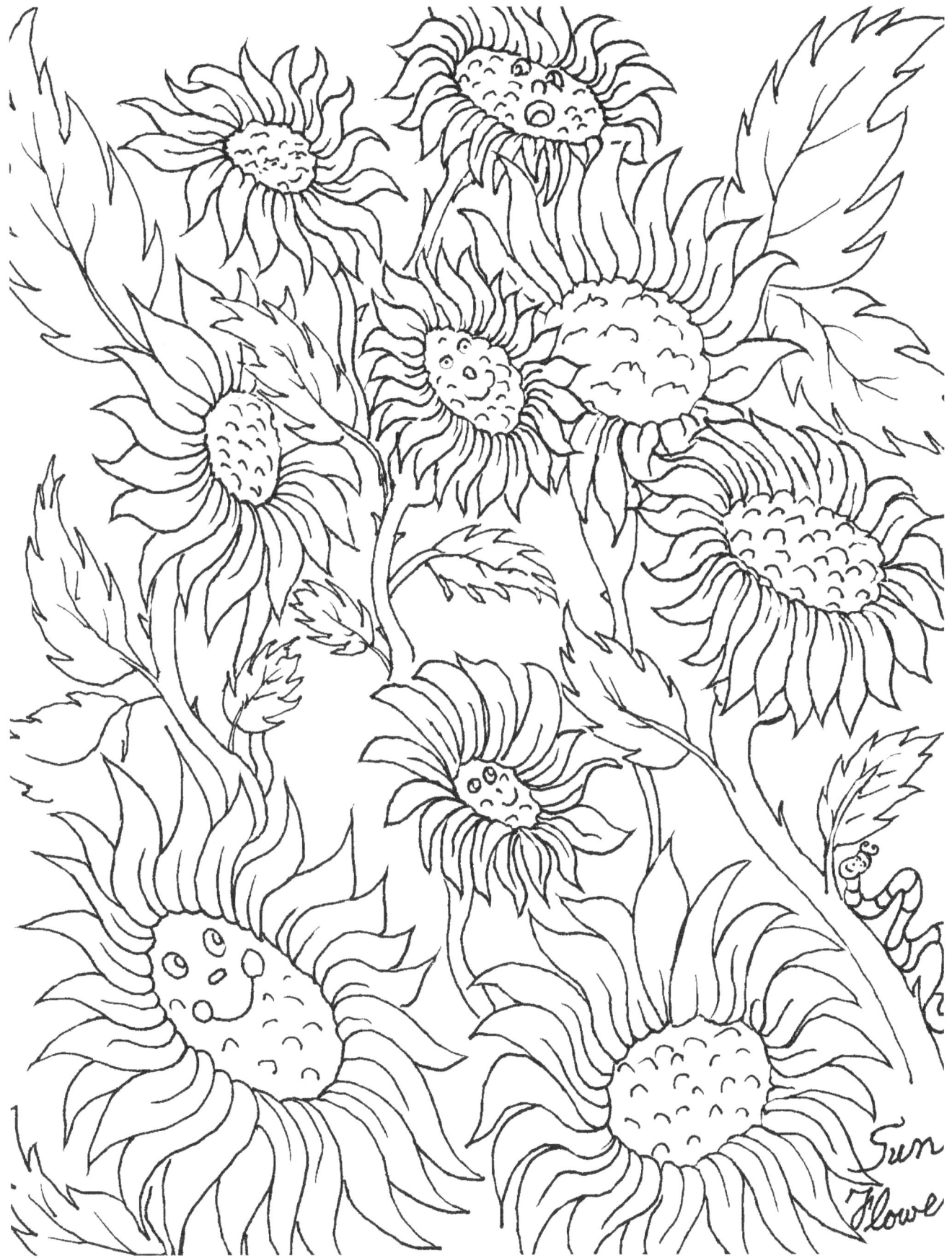

The Texas ponds are known for their water lilies and bull frogs.

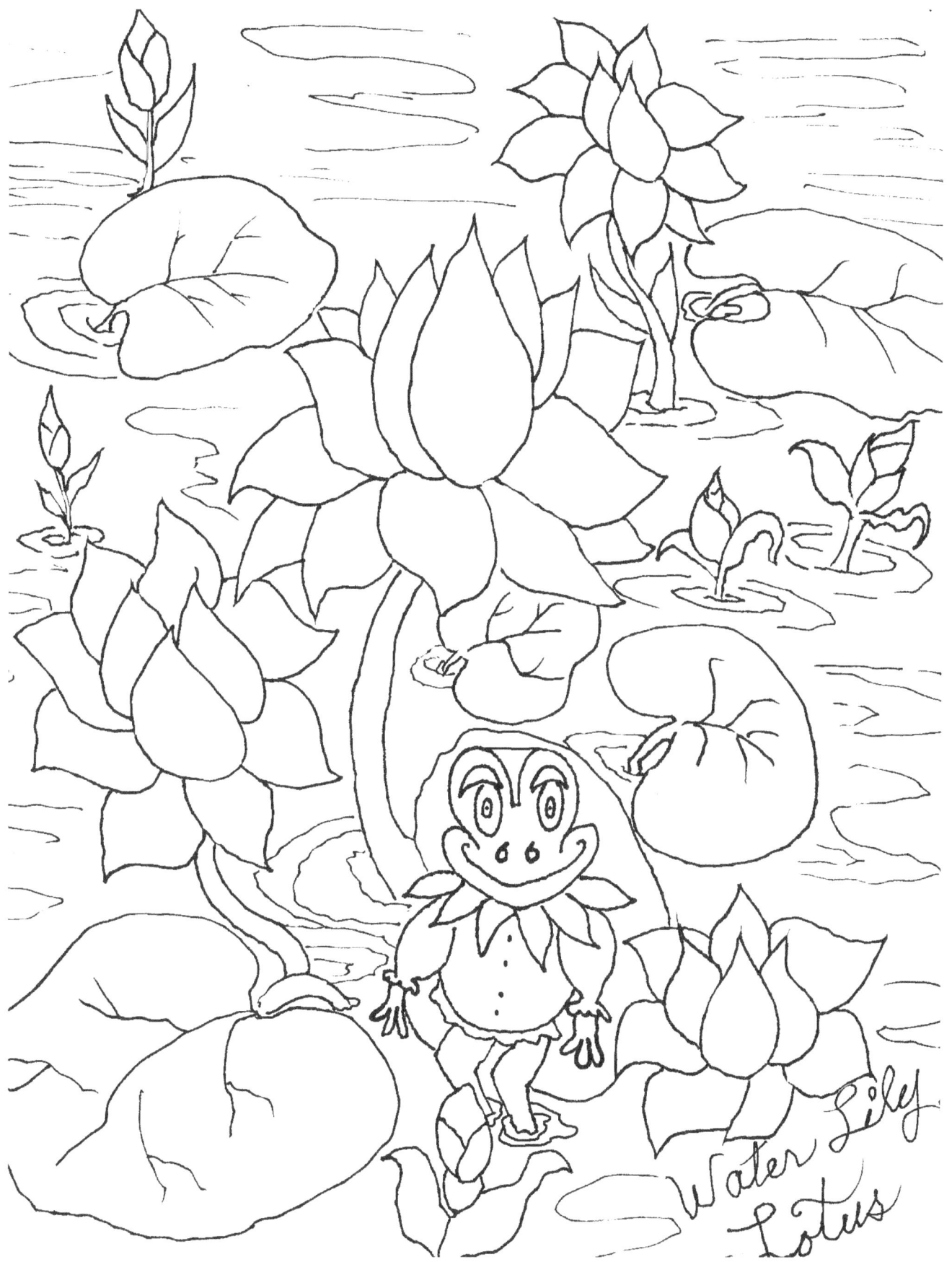

Water Lily
Lotus

In Texas, passion flowers are known as May pops because they pop out in early May, and are one of the edible wildflowers.

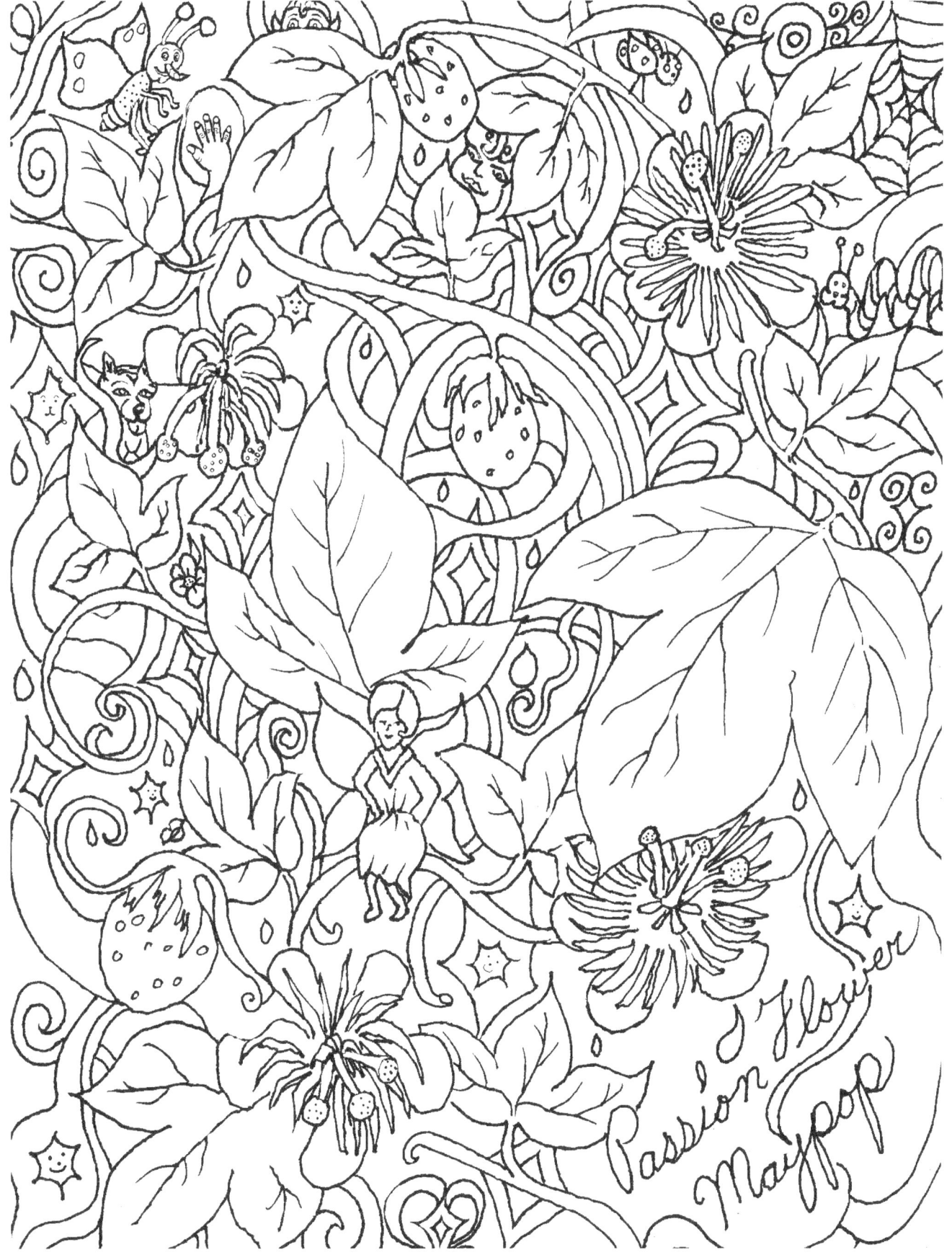

Around the cemeteries in Texas, you will find lots of rose bushes called Seven Sisters, which are heirloom roses that can be started from cuttings.

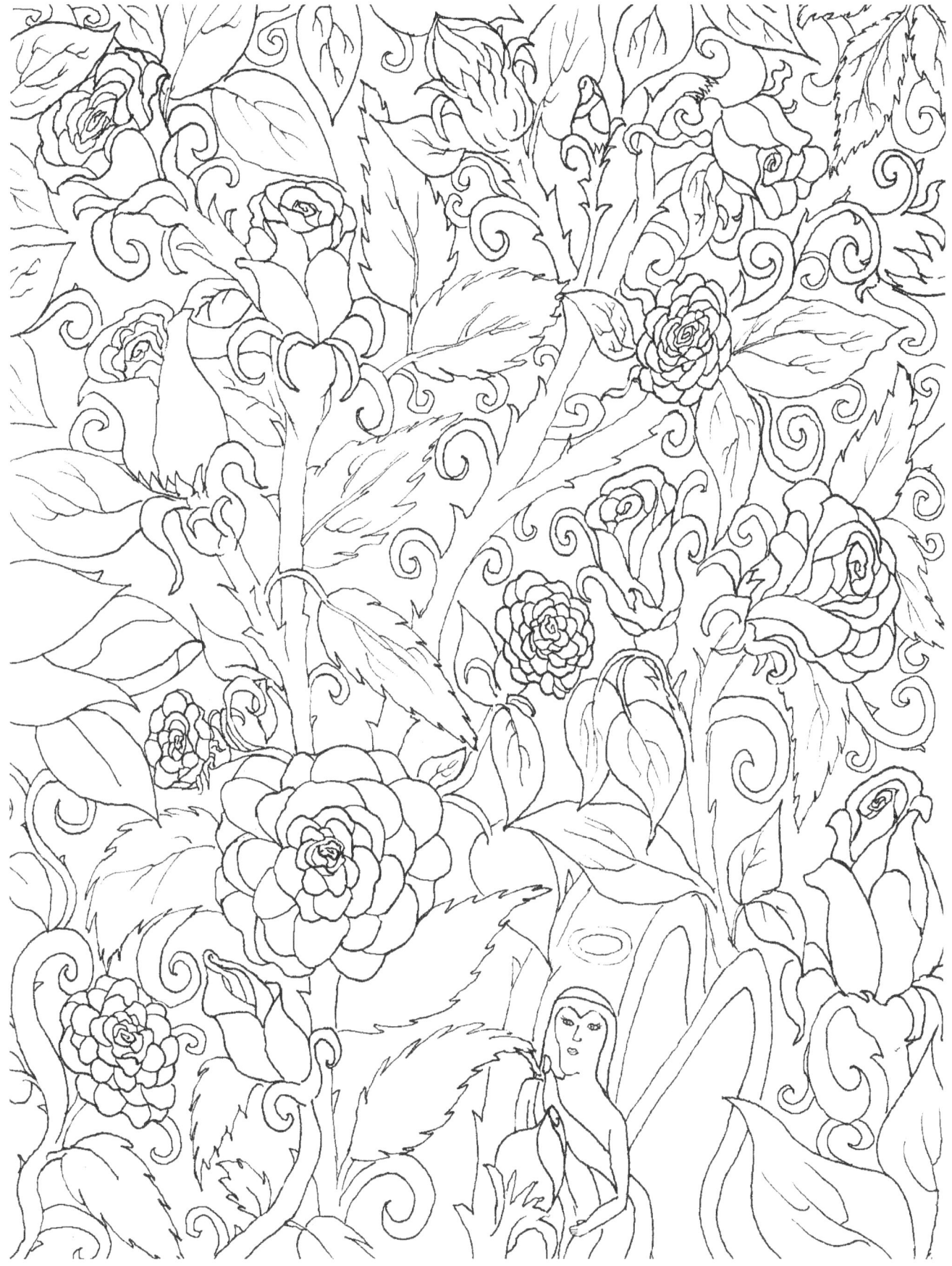

Have a relaxing day picking leaves in the woods of East Texas! How many kinds can you identify?

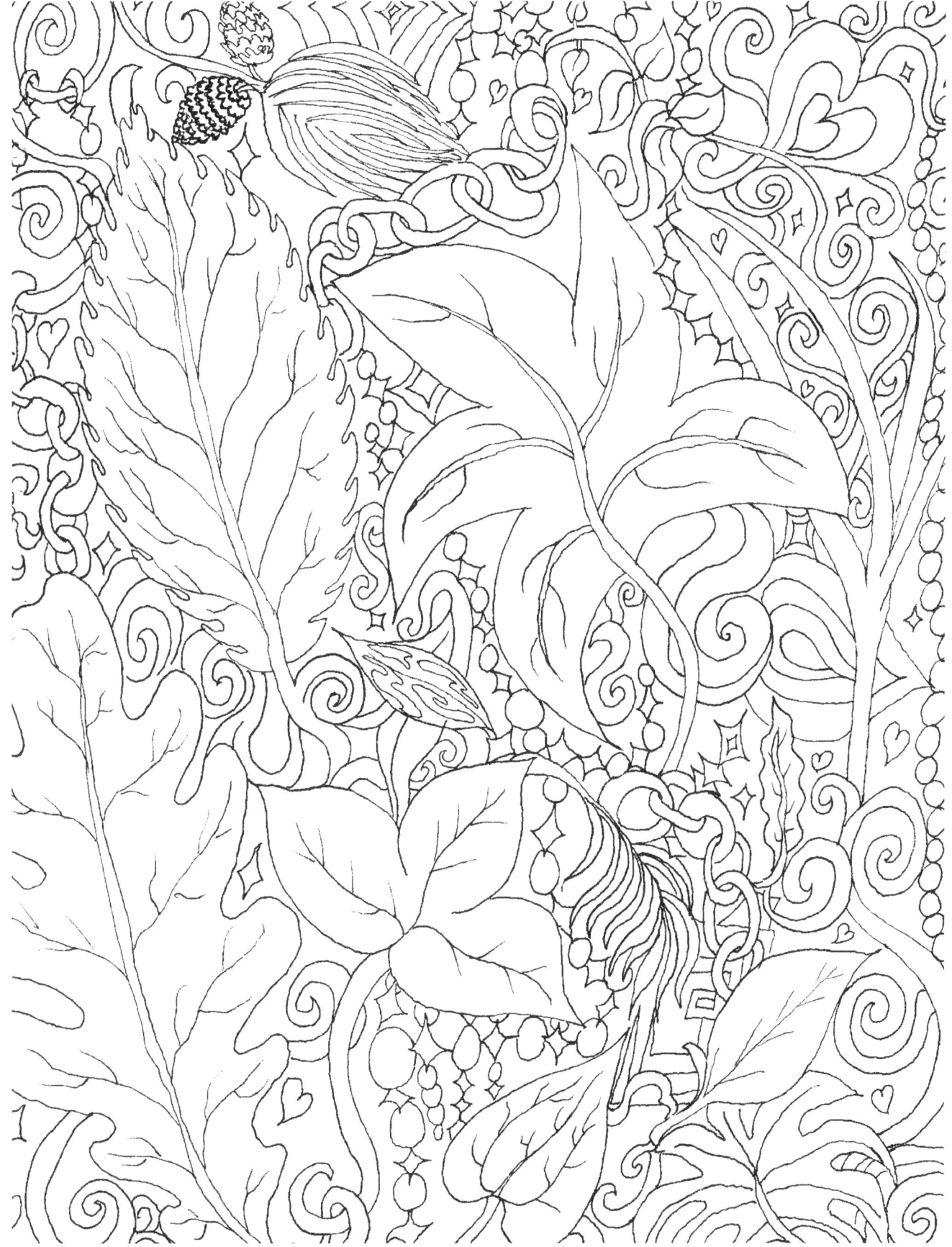

May Texas always be in your dreams!

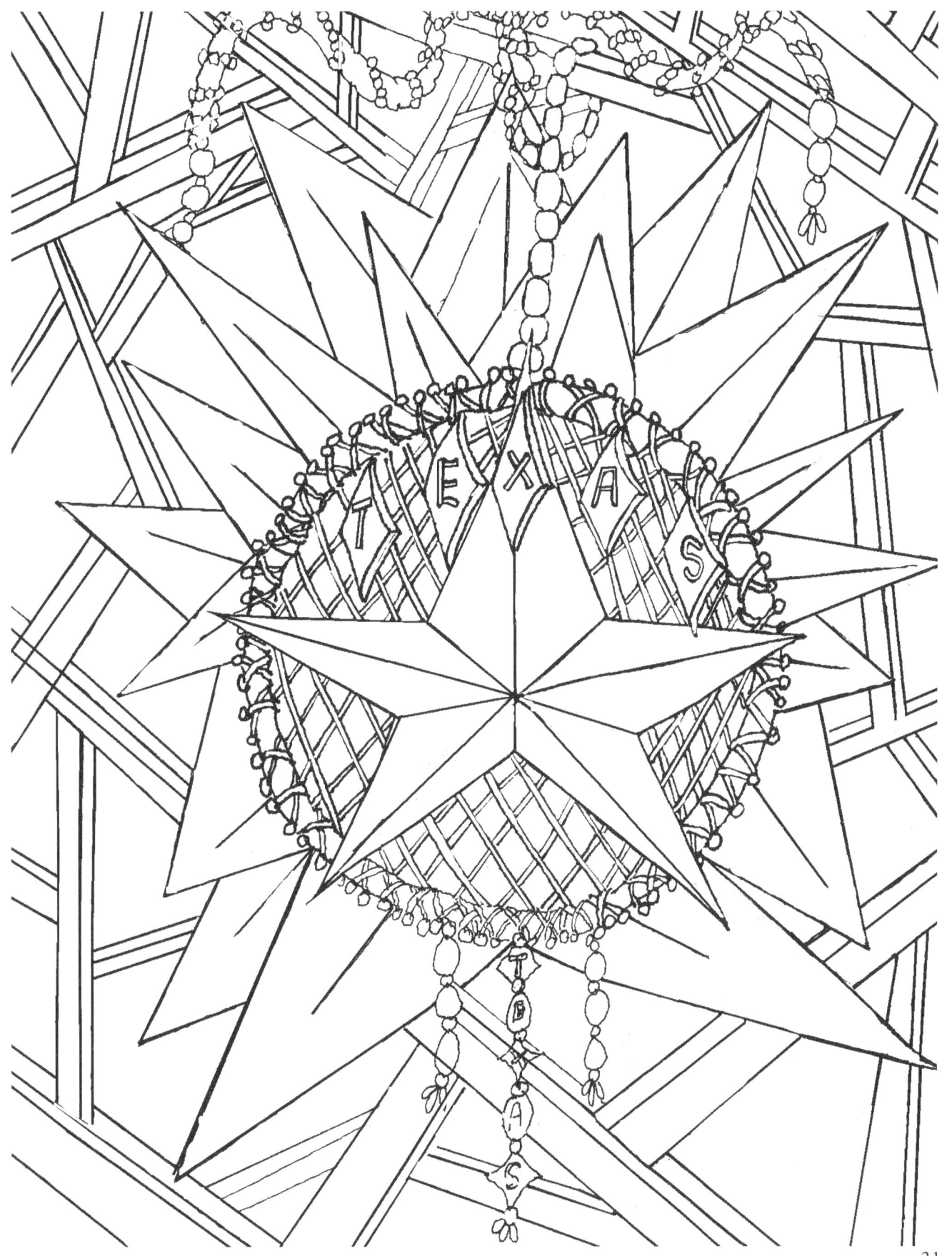

No trip to Texas would be complete without seeing armadillos and bluebonnets.

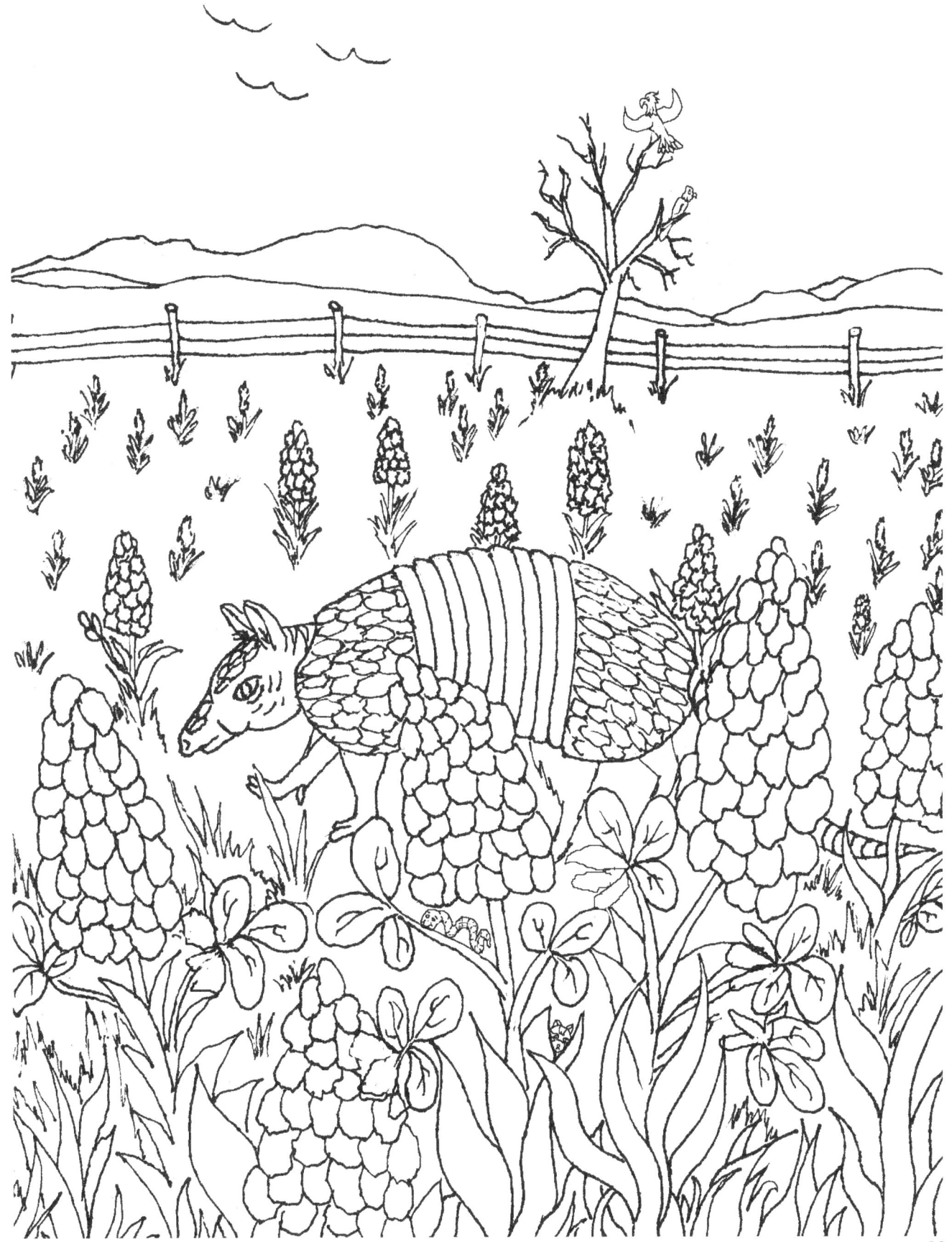

Texas is known for its dinosaur bones. We are still looking for our dragon bones!

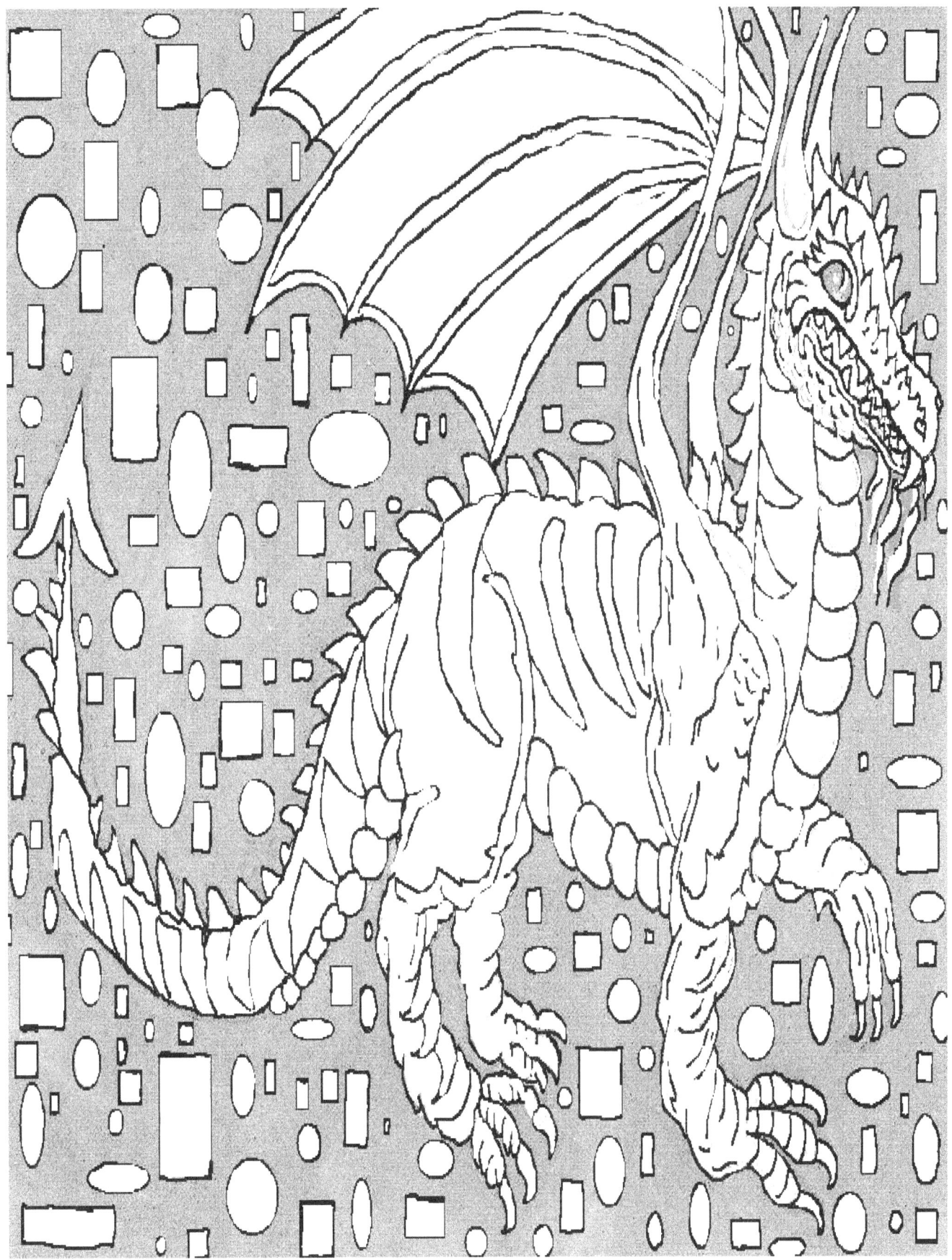

You know it's Easter time in East Texas
when you see the dogwoods bloom.

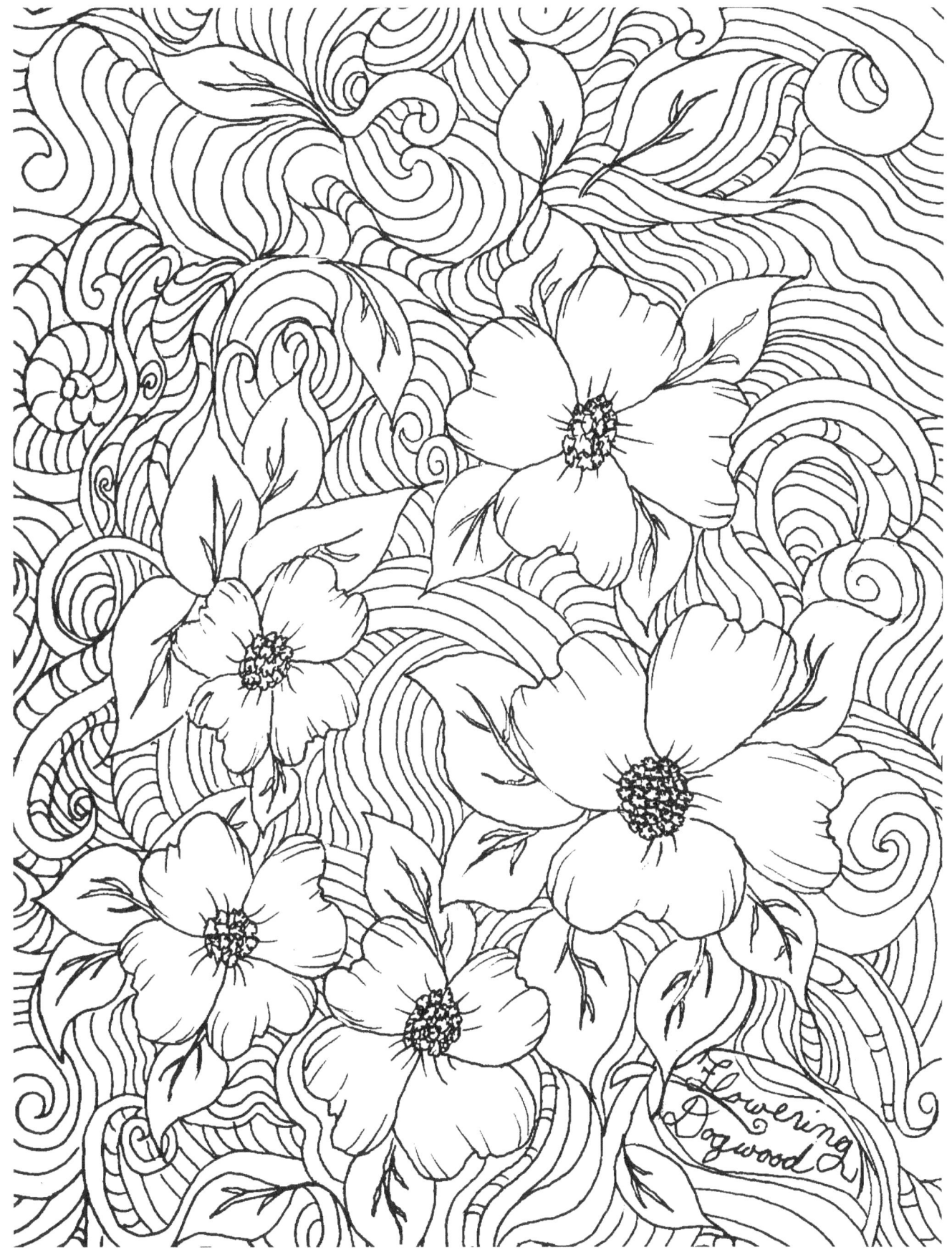

Flowering Dogwood

Riley Wiggles, a special Texan dog that starred in his own book, *Coming Home,* by Kristi Zimmerman, another special Texan!

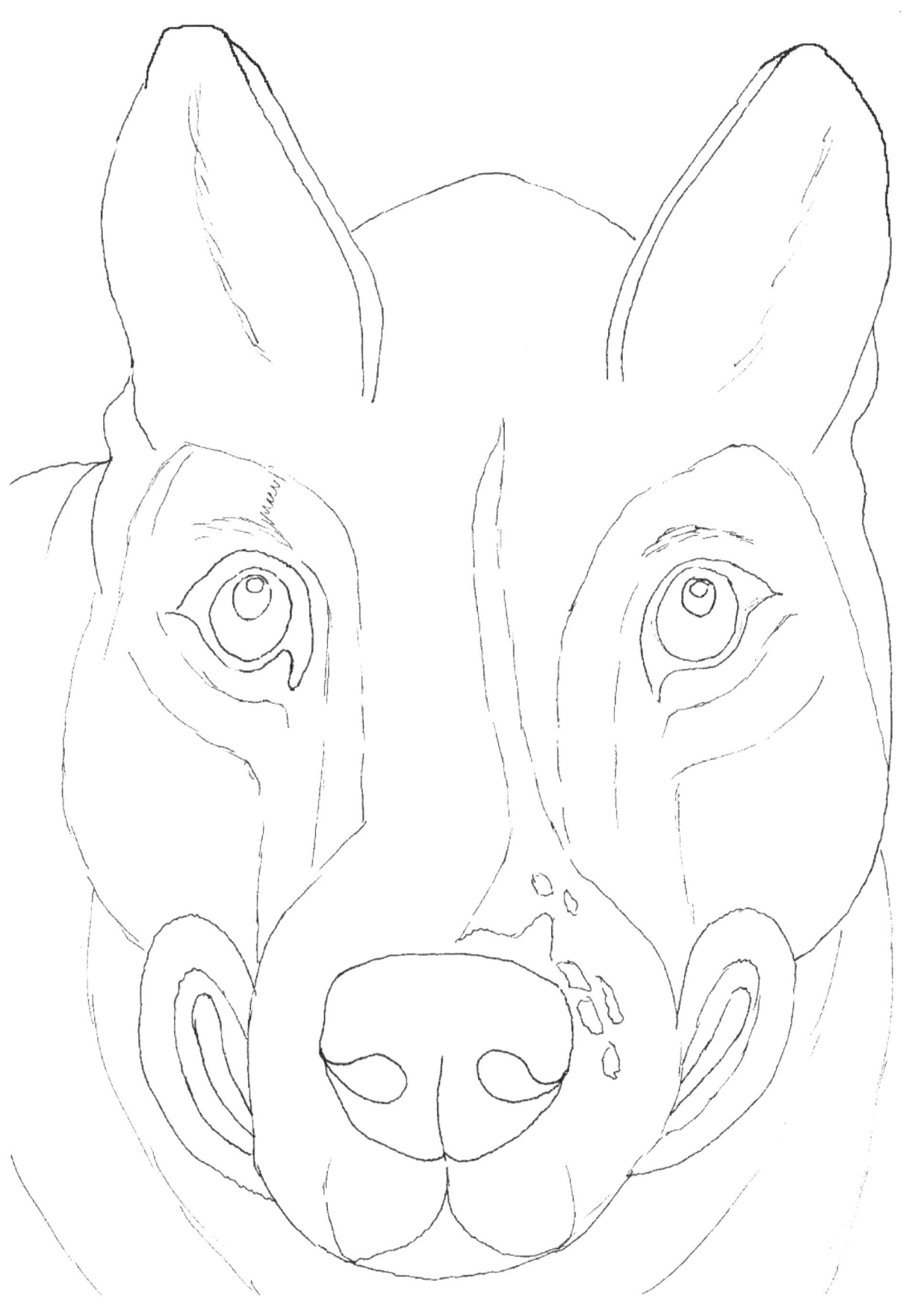

Wake up at the crack of dawn with your boots on to the sound of the rooster crow!

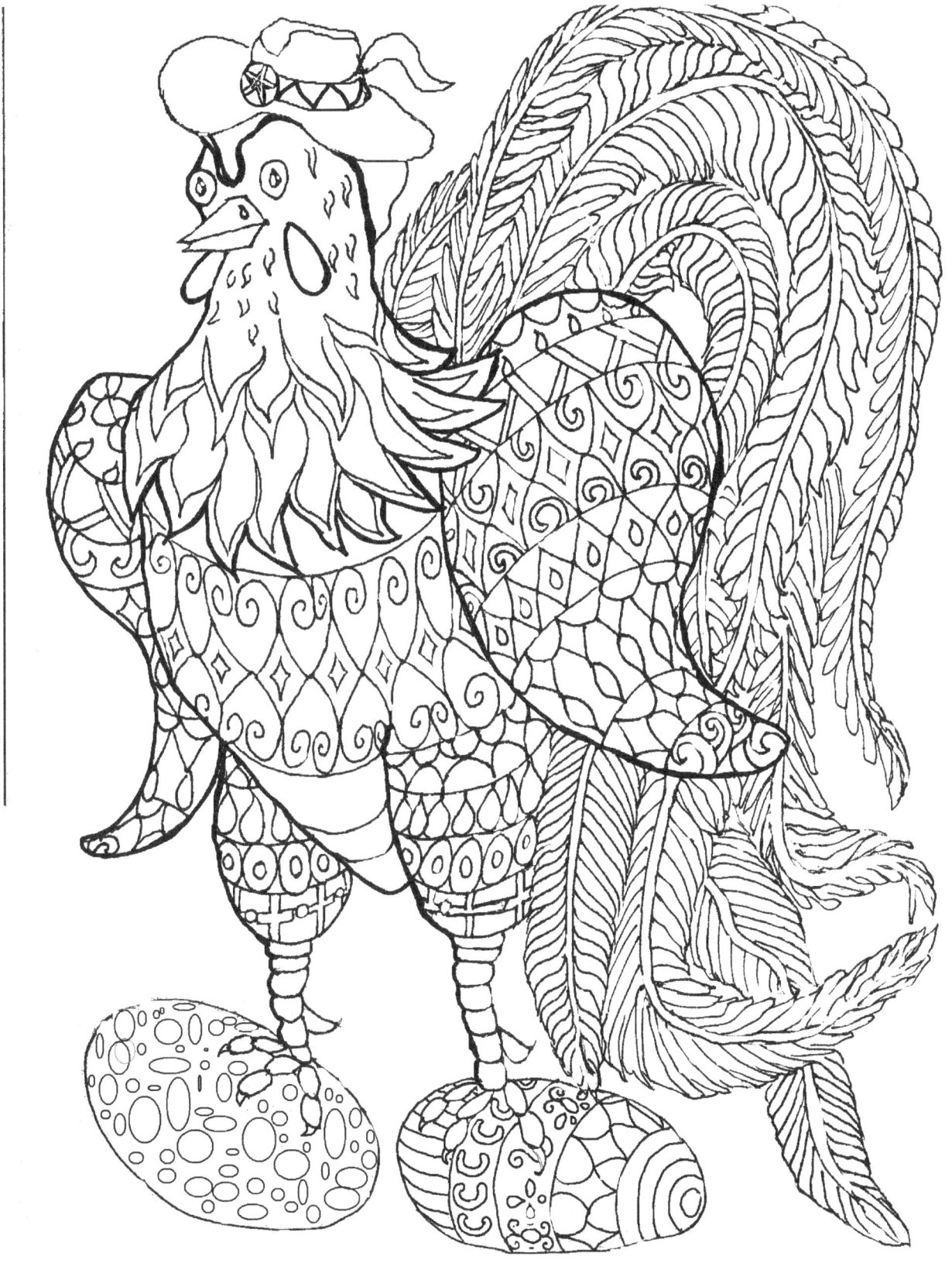

Sniffing out a little magic in the wildflowers!

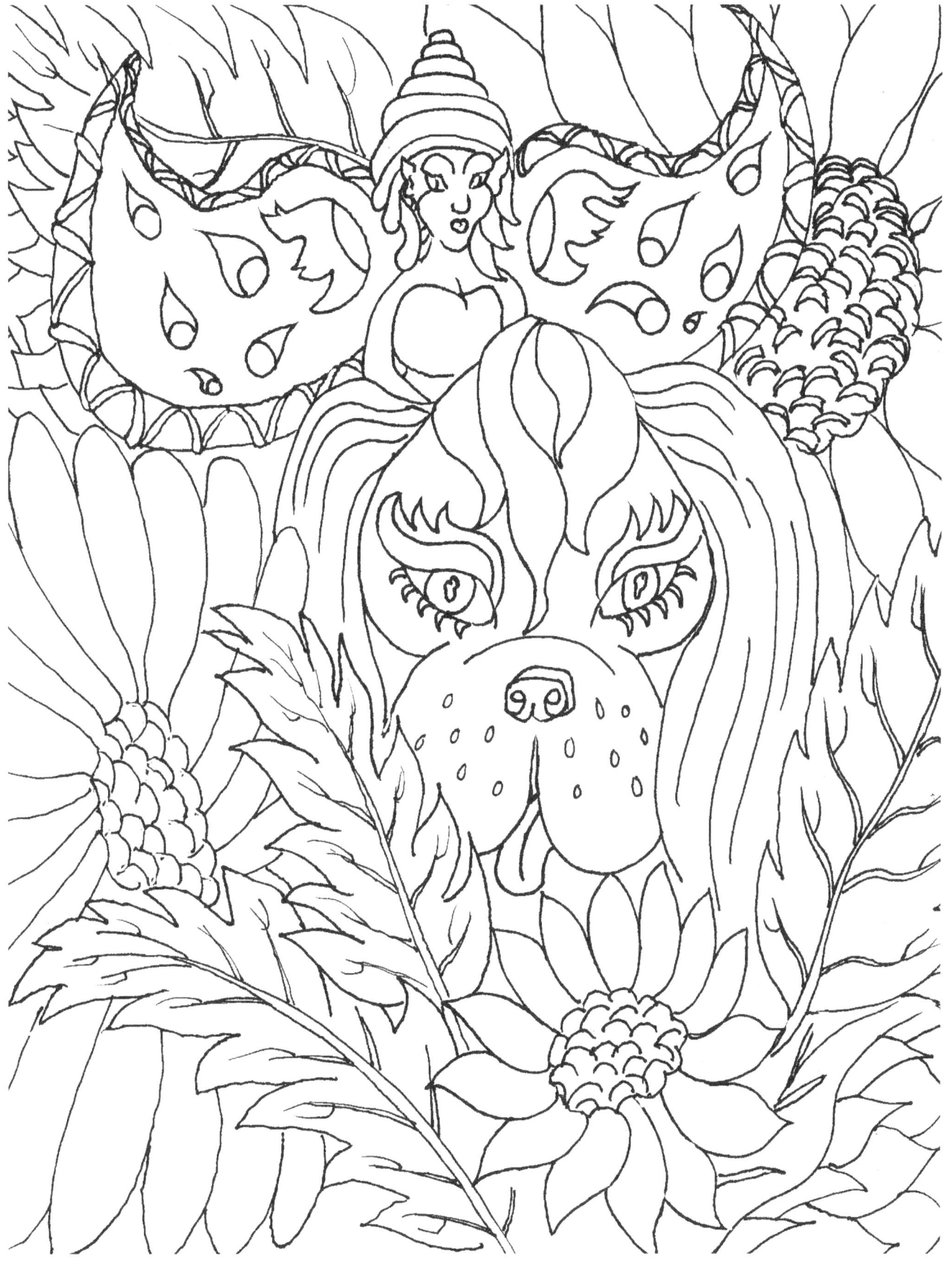

Be careful walking in the woods. The honeysuckles have spider webs.

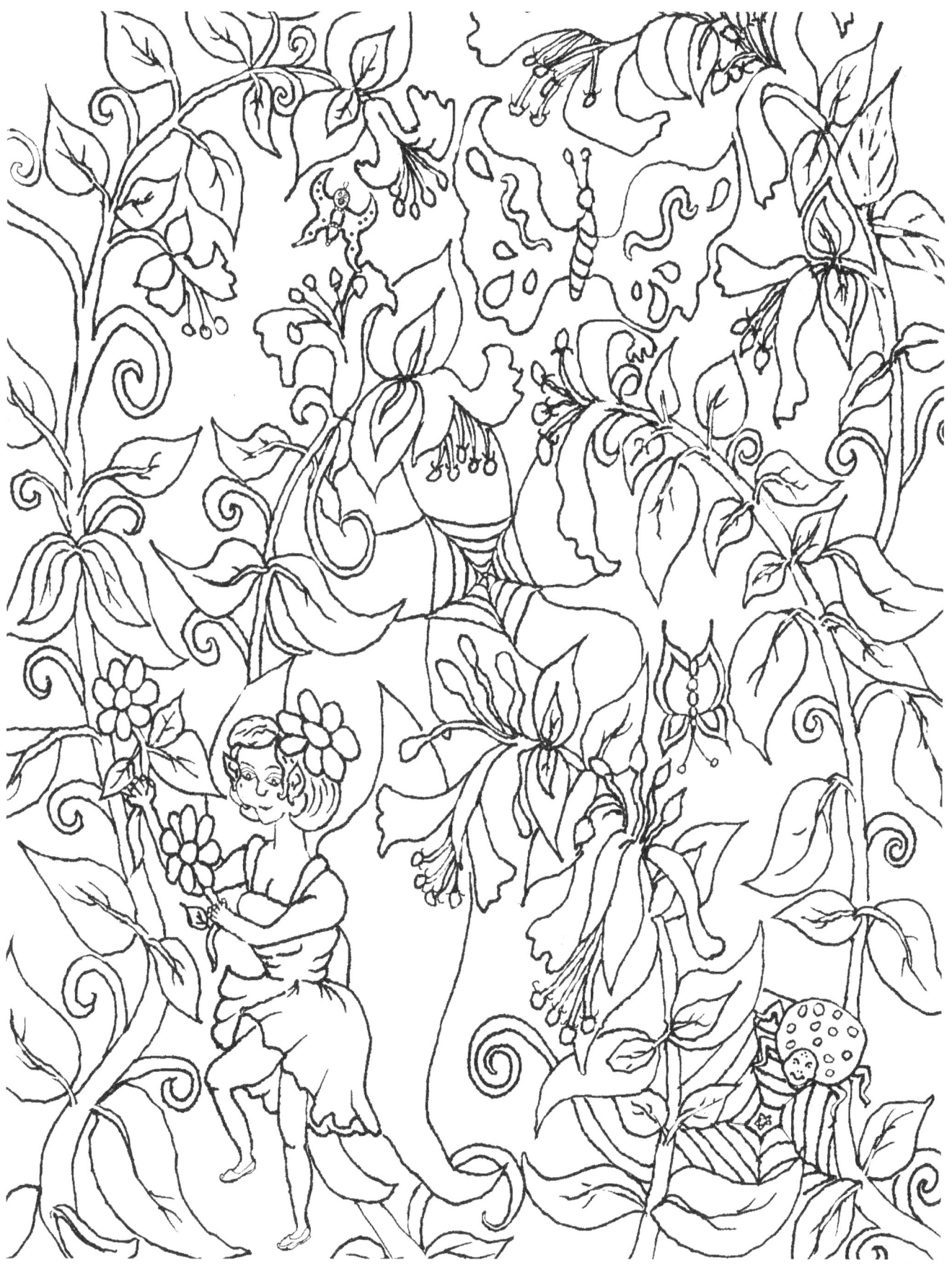

Texan's know how to have a good time, so come on down and have some fun! Bring your own root beer!

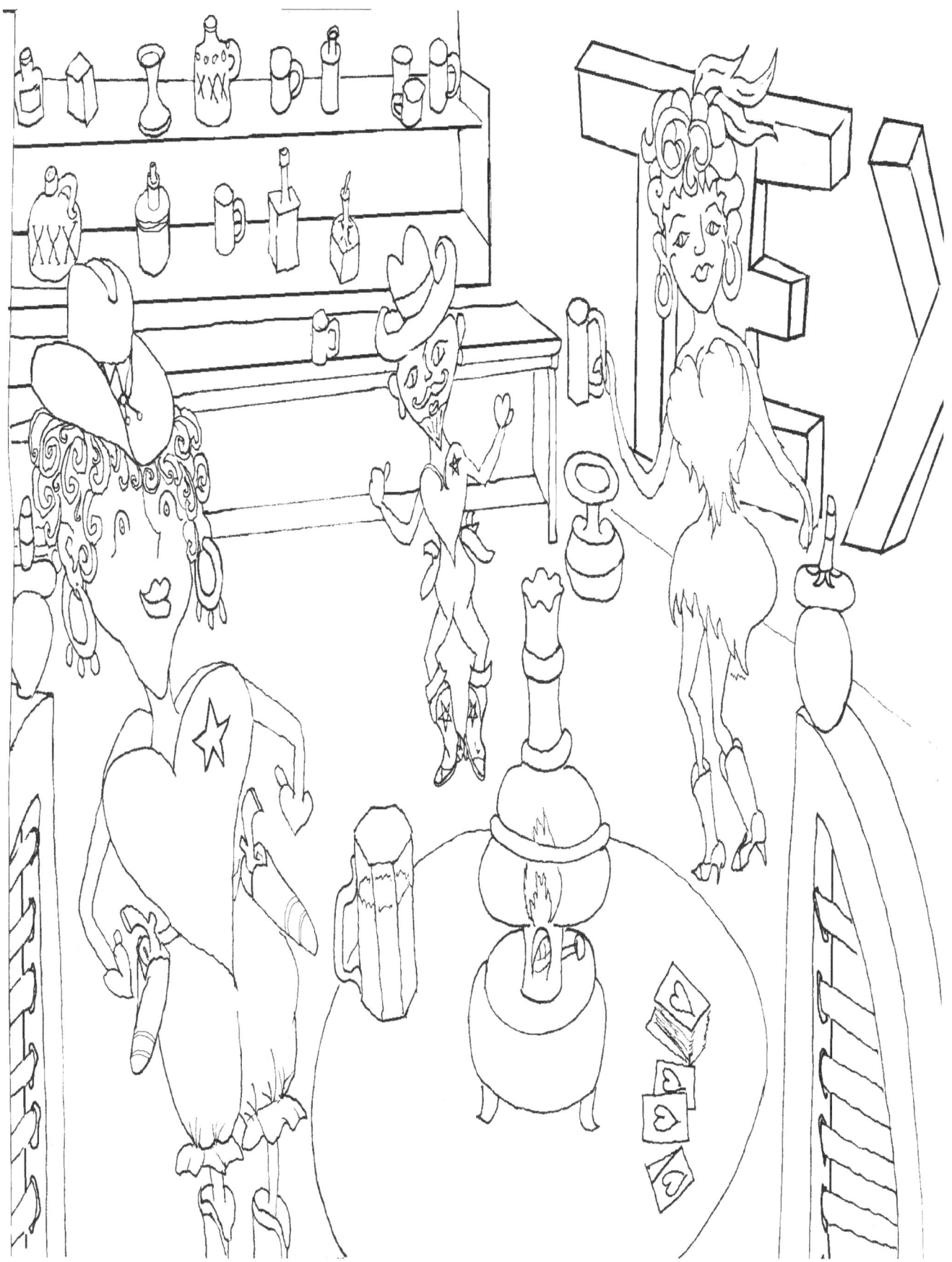

ABOUT THE AUTHOR

NORMA JEAN WAS BORN AND RAISED IN LOUISIANA AND HAS TRAVELED THE COUNTRY IN SEARCH OF ADVENTURE AND MAGIC. THROUGH MUCH OF HER LIFE, SHE HAS CREATED VARIOUS FORMS OF ART IN SCULPTURES, PAINTING, AND SKETCHES WHILE RAISING HER CHILDREN AND LOVING ALL GOD'S CREATURES.

www.ingramcontent.com/pod-product-compliance
Lightning Source LLC
Chambersburg PA
CBHW080606190526
45169CB00007B/2897